The Entrepreneur's Secret Code

Persuasion Magazine

Copyright © 2024 Michael McGavin

All rights reserved.

ISBN: 9798334866898

1-THE ENTREPRENEUR CLAIMS THE THRONE 1

2-THE ENTREPRENEUR IS FOCUSED ON HIS NEEDS 2

3-THE ENTREPRENEUR IS OBSESSED WITH MONEY 3

4-THE ENTREPRENEUR LETS THE WAVES CRASH AROUND HIM 4

5-THE ENTREPRENEUR KNOWS MONEY SOLVES MOST PROBLEMS 5

6-THE ENTREPRENEUR EXPLOITS PAIN 6

7-THE ENTREPRENEUR WELCOMES THIS BREAK DOWN 7

8-THE ENTREPRENEUR WORKS ON HIS ORIGIN STORY DAILY 7

9-THE ENTREPRENEUR IS A SPY 8

10-THE ENTREPRENEUR LOVES THIS SOUND 9

11-THE ENTREPRENEUR HAS ONLY PERMANENT INTERESTS 10

12-THE ENTREPRENEUR IS INDIFFERENT 11

13-EVERYTHING SERVES THE ENTREPRENEUR 12

14-THE ENTREPRENEUR IS RESPONSIBLE 13

15-THE ENTREPRENEUR ASKS THIS QUESTION 14

16-THE ENTREPRENEUR'S TWO SENTENCE OPERATING SYSTEM 15

17-THE ENTREPRENEUR LIVES A LIFE OF INDULGENCE 16

18-THE ENTREPRENEUR EMBRACES RAPID CHANGE 17

19-THE ENTREPRENEUR KNOWS MONEY BUYS HAPPINESS 18

20-THE ENTREPRENEUR RELISHES HIS VICTORIES 19

21-THE ENTREPRENEUR UNDERSTANDS THE STAKES 20

22-THE ENTREPRENEUR UNDERSTANDS THIS BUSINESS FORMULA 21

23-THE ENTREPRENEUR MAINTAINS CLARITY 23

24-THE ENTREPRENEUR KNOWS LIFE IS ABOUT SURVIVAL OF THE FITTEST 24

25-THE ENTREPRENEUR BELIEVES IN HIS OWN CAUSE 25

26-THE ENTREPRENEUR KNOWS HOW EASY IT IS TO FALL ASLEEP 26

27-THE ENTREPRENEUR ACTS WHEN OTHERS HESITATE 27

28-THE ENTREPRENEUR WALKS THROUGH THE OPEN DOOR 28

29-THE ENTREPRENEUR CREATES A NEW REALITY 29

30-THE ENTREPRENEUR KNOWS PEOPLE ONLY WANT GOOD NEWS 30

31-THE ENTREPRENEUR DOESN'T TRY 31

32-THE ENTREPRENEURS IS ALWAYS SELLING 32

33-THE ENTREPRENEUR CAN PLAY A ROLE 33

34-THE ENTREPRENEUR KNOWS SUCCESS IS THE BEST REVENGE 34

35-THE ENTREPRENEUR LETS OTHER PEOPLE HAVE THEIR MORALITY 35

36-THE ENTREPRENEUR CULTIVATES HIS ENERGY 36

37-WHAT IS THE ENTREPRENEUR'S PROJECT? 37

38-THE ENTREPRENEUR DOES NOT GO TO AN EMPTY WELL 38

39-THE ENTREPRENEUR WANTS EVERYONE TO BE AN ENTREPRENEUR 39

40-THE ENTREPRENEUR IS WARY OF FAME 40

41-THE ENTREPRENEUR KEEPS HIS LIFE SIMPLE 41

42-THE ENTREPRENEUR CONTROLS HIS TIME 41

43-THE ENTREPRENEUR SEEKS TO BECOME A MASTER 42

44-THE ENTREPRENEUR IS IN ONE BUSINESS 43

45-THE ENTREPRENEUR USES THIS 3-STAGE ANTIDOTE FOR FRUSTRATION 44

46-THE ENTREPRENEUR ALWAYS TAKES ANOTHER STEP 45

47-THE ENTREPRENEUR USES ANGER 46

48-THE ENTREPRENEUR NEVER FIGHTS THE TAPE 48

49-THE ENTREPRENEUR KNOWS IDENTITY IS STRONGER THAN DESIRE 48

50-THE ENTREPRENEUR RESTS WHEN HE IS WEARY 49

51-THE ENTREPRENEUR CAN SMILE WHEN HE'S GETTING SCREWED 51

52-THE ENTREPRENEUR WILL SHARE WHEN OTHERS ARE READY 52

53-THE ENTREPRENEUR ASKS HIMSELF THIS QUESTION 52

54-THE ENTREPRENEUR KNOWS MOST ARE STUCK IN PERMANENT CHILDHOOD 54

55-THE ENTREPRENEUR SETS HIS OWN STANDARD 55

56-THE ENTREPRENEUR IS SELF-RELIANT 56

57-THE ENTREPRENEUR KNOWS MEN ARE BORN IN BATTLE 57

58-THE ENTREPRENEUR KNOWS PEOPLE ALREADY LIVE IN AUGMENTED REALITY 59

59-THE ENTREPRENEUR CAPITALIZES ON THE ERRORS OF HIS ADVERSARIES 60

60-THE ENTREPRENEUR IS MENTALLY TOUGH 61

61-THE ENTREPRENEUR KNOWS MAN IS GOD ON EARTH 62

62-THE ENTREPRENEUR UNDERSTANDS THE FOLLY OF WORKING FOR MONEY 63

63-THE ENTREPRENEUR CULTIVATES CONFIDENCE 64

64-THE ENTREPRENEUR KNOWS GANG ACTIVITY WHEN HE SEES IT 65

65-THE ENTREPRENEUR WORSHIPS NO HEROES 65

66-THE ENTREPRENEUR UNDERSTANDS THE CONSEQUENCES OF FAILURE 66

67-THE ENTREPRENEUR KNOWS HE WILL BE DEAD FOR A MILLION YEARS 67

68-THE ENTREPRENEUR IS NO ACCIDENT 68

69-THE ENTREPRENEUR KNOWS FREEDOM ISN'T "FREE" 69

70-THE ENTREPRENEUR KNOWS SOCIETAL RAGE IS BORN FROM ENVY 70

71-THE ENTREPRENEUR REMEMBERS HIMSELF DAILY 71

72-THE ENTREPRENEUR ASSESSES HIS PROGRESS 72

73-THE ENTREPRENEUR MOWS HIS LAWN AND SHOVELS THE SIDEWALK 72

74-THE ENTREPRENEUR DOES NOT GET THROWN UNDER THE BUS 73

75-THE ENTREPRENEUR DOESN'T THINK HE'S GREEDY 75

76-THE ENTREPRENEUR BREATHES 76

77-THE ENTREPRENEUR KNOWS THIS CONTEST IS DECIDED DAILY 77

78-THE ENTREPRENEUR DOES NOT BEG FOR WHAT IS HIS 78

79-THE ENTREPRENEUR CONTEMPLATES HIS BEST INTEREST 79

80-THE ENTREPRENEUR DOES NOT SEEK APPROVAL 80

81-THE ENTREPRENEUR FORGES THIS PATH TO FREEDOM 82

82-THE ENTREPRENEUR DETERMINES HIS VALUE 83

83-THE ENTREPRENEUR EATS WHAT HE KILLS 84

84-THE ENTREPRENEUR IS THE ONLY GOD IN TOWN 85

85-TO THE ENTREPRENEUR BELONGS THE WORLD 86

86-THE ENTREPRENEUR KNOWS FEAR IS A CONSTRUCT 87

87-THE ENTREPRENEUR EXERCISES HIS POWER IN THE MARKETPLACE 88

88-THE ENTREPRENEUR IS A MAN OF ACTION 90

89-THE ENTREPRENEUR CLOSES THE GAP 91

90-THE ENTREPRENEUR IS OUTCOME ORIENTED 92

1-The Entrepreneur claims the throne

The Entrepreneur shows up and declares himself whatever he decides.

He has prepared himself internally to be the thing. Then he is the thing.

He doesn't question it because it has become his truth.

Therefore no one else questions it.

He never feels like a fraud because he knows everything is arbitrary. He could be this thing or another thing - either one is a result of his choice.

So the Entrepreneur chooses to be the thing that gives him the most pleasure and the least pain.

Everything flows from that - especially the way others respond to him and give him what he has decided.

And the Entrepreneur keeps showing up, simply being the thing he has decided - CEO, celebrity or master chef.

For budding Entrepreneurs the key is preparation - understanding that you are the only authority in your life and have all the power to make your own decisions over what is good or bad, desirable or to be avoided.

After spending the time to own this truth, from the inside out, you can claim anything in the outside world.

You become the Entrepreneur simply by showing up with that authority.

2-The Entrepreneur is focused on his needs

For the Entrepreneur, there is only himself.

He may need money, or peace.

The Entrepreneur knows he can give himself whatever he needs at any moment – because he is willing to focus only on that.

He knows that if he is worried, he is not focused.

He grants himself peace by vacating that weakness.

The Entrepreneur knows that worry is an inheritance from voices that are no longer present.

When the Entrepreneur needs money, he takes action.

He knows that if he is not taking action that is another impediment that came from outside himself.

The more he focuses on what he needs the more the Entrepreneur understands he has it within himself to grant his own wishes.

Anything that is not what he wants is a lack of focus.

Lack of focus is a handicap that others attempted to breed into him.

The Entrepreneur has decided to focus and take control of his own power.

And that is most of the battle.

3-The Entrepreneur is obsessed with money

There's a simple reason why the Entrepreneur begins, lives and ends his day working on money.

The Entrepreneur understands that money creates the container within which he can live the life he desires.

The amount of money he acquires determines what type of container he gets to enjoy.

If it's small, flimsy and leaking he will live a life of constant stress.

If it is large and sturdy and abundant and luxurious he will get to live a life of enjoyment and free from worry.

The Entrepreneur understand no one is going to build this container for him.

The Entrepreneur understands that other people want the same things he wants.

He may find allies and he may find competitors.

But he keeps his mind and his actions directed on protecting the container in which he lives his life.

That container is made of money. Without that container there is no life.

Without the money that creates that container there is no life.

Is it any wonder the Entrepreneur is obsessed with money?

4-The Entrepreneur lets the waves crash around him

The world is turmoil - at least as long as humans are spinning the wheel.

There are wars and weather, famines and plagues.

The Entrepreneur can look at a single day of news and understand this is the way it has always been and always will be.

So he is unbothered by whatever happens to flash on the screen because he knows it will pass.

The Entrepreneur enjoys his time - and if he can benefit from the turmoil in his corner of the world, that is also the way it has always been.

If he needs to step out of the line of fire - when there is nothing to be gained - he is content to watch the show.

His first and only obligation is to himself - so he lets the waves and the cries crash around him.

They are not his concern.

5-The Entrepreneur knows money solves most problems

Many of the so-called stresses of daily life for average people are simply having to work too many hours for too little money in the face of financial obligations that are too high.

The Entrepreneur knows that more money dissolves most of these daily stresses.

He will spend some to diminish such stresses but his mind and his productive energy is directed toward making the money necessary to making them simply disappear.

He also understands that most others have given up or refuse to acknowledge this truth - and there may be a way to sell something to take their minds off money stress, if only for a few moments.

While others may be content to settle for small distractions from the real stress of not having enough money, the Entrepreneur understands the true stakes.

Without enough money, life is small and dark.

With more than enough money, life takes on the air of

happiness and freedom that makes it worth living.

The Entrepreneur knows he can deliver this to himself and makes this his aim.

6-The Entrepreneur exploits pain

This is obvious to anyone who explores becoming an Entrepreneur.

When you decide that you're going to eliminate the pain points from your life you understand that other people will pay good money to have their own pains diminished.

And the best research is to begin with yourself.

What are the most painful things you are experiencing?

How can you eliminate them?

Or how did you eliminate some pain points already?

Figure out a way to repeat this process in a product or service and you will profit from pain.

And it will be what is known as a clean transaction.

That is, you have provided a true service to a customer or audience.

Without cheating or manipulating. This is a simple business model that you can implement today.

What is your greatest pain? What have you done to fix it, or what would you need to do in order to be rid of it?

Provide that and you'll have a million like you offering you cash.

7-The Entrepreneur welcomes this break down

As the Entrepreneur advances in developing his mental faculties a schism in his personality will occur.

He will see his previous self as something that was manufactured by his surroundings.

It will feel separate from him and he will feel like a snake that has just shed its skin.

If he is wise he will understand that the person he has become is yet another skin that will eventually be shed.

Therefore he continues to hone his faculties - to view his life as something under his own authority, that his actions are directed toward only his own goals and his satisfaction comes from his own power.

As he continues cultivating this ability he will assume even greater levels of mastery.

He will only stop growing when he stops concentrating on his own unique life.

8-The Entrepreneur works on his origin story daily

The Entrepreneur reminds himself every day that his good is his only cause. That his needs are his only concern and that his opinion is the only one that matters.

He is always aware that he is the only one responsible for the outcomes he produces.

He contemplates that he has this one life to do with as he pleases and this idea lifts his spirits.

The Entrepreneur is in control because he was granted control at birth. And he works to maintain and strengthen this control.

He produces for himself the freedom and profit and ease that he desires by taking the action that only he can take.

The Entrepreneur reminds himself daily that he is unique and a power unto himself.

9-The Entrepreneur is a spy

The Entrepreneur takes note of foreign spies who have infiltrated societies - that they were trained like actors to play a role.

But the Entrepreneur serves no foreign power - but his own.

He understands his childhood beliefs were gifted to him like old luggage. He has thrown them aside.

He has chosen to pick from all the options available to him and invented a few of his own. He knows how to blend in and when to stand out.

The Entrepreneur has trained himself to live in the circles he desires, by adopting social cues and language patterns.

But he knows better than to believe it.

Because tomorrow he may decide to be something else - by necessity or whim - and then he. will adopt a new set of beliefs and behaviors, always shifting, always serving his own cause – and enjoying each skin he wears throughout his life.

10-The Entrepreneur loves this sound

The sound of the cash register ringing.

It is music that lifts the Entrepreneur's spirit and puts a smile on his face.

The sound of cash changing hands. The feeling of it going into his pocket.

Even digital transactions make noise - when the Entrepreneur sees it he laughs with joy.

The Entrepreneur loves to make this money-making music every single day.

It lights up whatever section of his brain gives him joy and happiness and makes him feel alive.

He doesn't need to know the science because he

experiences the sensation.

And the more money-making music he makes the easier it becomes to hum that tune.

It becomes a background music to his life and makes his way easy and light.

11-The Entrepreneur has only permanent interests

Allies and enemies are temporary for the Entrepreneur.

Only his interest remains constant.

Or shall we say only his interest in his own interests remain constant.

His objectives may change but he is always about satisfying his own needs.

There will be times when people oppose him and there will be times when others help him.

They are means to an end and temporary.

He is friendly and even at all times.

Once his objective is achieved his allies may dessert him or his competitors may join his cause.

That too is temporary.

Yet he is not above understanding the need for close relations.

He relies on his projection of self to cultivate his allies and keep his enemies on their toes.

This engenders respect, which to the Entrepreneur is more important than friendship or fear.

12-The Entrepreneur is indifferent

The Entrepreneur's goals are to maximize his pleasure and minimize pain.

He works for money because he knows that is the medium by which pleasure is obtained.

And having money means he can avoid the pains the majority have to endure.

But he also works on his mind - he knows that for the cost of a little effort and no money at all - he can live a cheerful life and avoid pain simply by having no concern for the world.

That means he remains indifferent to what other people do, what other people say or think.

He doesn't bother himself with getting worked up about injustice or fraud.

Those are the actions of others and they're doing as they wish.

He knows he has no control over the actions of others, therefore anything but indifference means he is succumbing to their actions even though he is not the intended victim.

He also knows that when he remains true to himself - increases his wealth and his own happiness that others may benefit.

And when he does ever give thought to benefiting someone other than himself, he knows this is something he is willing to give away without expecting anything in return.

13-Everything serves the Entrepreneur

The Entrepreneur has taken command of his existence.

He sees everything around him as inert - just things in the reality around him.

Nothing has any power over him.

Though there are facts to consider.

But these facts have no power.

Therefore the Entrepreneur decides to consider every fact as something that is there for his benefit.

This is a psychological shift that enables him to remain in command of his life.

He works with the idea, "everything serves me".

The Entrepreneur is able to easily handle challenges

and maintain a positive attitude with this idea.

He sees his life as it truly is - a wonderful experience through a reality that is always within his control.

The Entrepreneur's life is a reality where everything serves him.

14-The Entrepreneur is responsible

No matter what the condition the Entrepreneur takes 100% responsibility.

If he has enjoyed a glorious victory, he basks in its warmth.

If he is delivered a setback, he accepts responsibility for dealing with the situation.

If he was born without a father, he accepts this reality. And figures out how to parent himself.

If he has household bills above his means, he figures out a way to generate more revenue.

He understands that while some circumstances are enjoyable and others challenging he is the only one who is going to do anything about it.

And yes he will linger in his enjoyment because he knows difficulties are part of the journey.

So he takes responsibility for the entirety of his experience.

He is the one who has made it, he is the one who takes action, he is the one who will make something out of nothing and turn dross into gold.

He is always aware that he is center stage in his own life - that he is the architect, the actor and the audience of his own story.

15-The Entrepreneur asks this question

Whenever meeting someone new, the Entrepreneur asks, "where does your money come from?"

He does not ask this question out loud.

The Entrepreneur, when interacting with others, figures out the source of their income.

Because people behave almost entirely based on their economic situation he knows the answer to this question tells him everything he needs to understand about the other.

He knows that the words they say, the act they put on is just a cover for their economic base.

If he meets a poor person who acts like an animal he understands. They live from day to day scratching for the next meal and hoping not to get robbed.

If he meets someone well to do he wants to know where their resources come from. If they stole it, by either legal or illegal means, he is delighted.

He knows what he is dealing with and will appeal to their true nature.

If they earned it he is equally delighted. He knows that they have a value system to which he can appeal.

The Entrepreneur also asks himself where his own money comes from.

And the answer is always the same: "my money comes from myself."

16-The Entrepreneur's two sentence operating system

1. The Entrepreneur recognizes only himself.

2. The Entrepreneur rejects anything outside of himself

These two ideas form the basis for the Entrepreneur's mode of living.

He works on them diligently because they are contrary to the conditioning meant to create slaves.

He thinks about his own needs and his own desires and how he's going to get them.

He brushes aside any notion of what others think is right or possible or even allowable.

This last part, about rejecting what other people think he is allowed to do is answered when he refers back to the first idea.

That because he recognizes only himself he knows anything is allowable for him.

Further by lifelong contemplation he comes to understand that anything he wishes is his right.

Because when he recognizes only himself and rejects anything outside of himself he comes to his truth – that he alone is the authority over his life.

That he decides what he wants, what he must have and how to go about getting it.

These two ideas which give birth to the awareness of his authority are the basis of the Entrepreneur's freedom.

17-The Entrepreneur lives a life of indulgence

The Entrepreneur seeks any pleasure he desires.

He indulges himself in delights and luxury. If he decides he wants to be lazy he does as he wishes.

If he decides he wants to be wealthy he gets what he wants.

He enjoys the pastimes and the gadgets the world has to offer.

If they exist it is his right to have them.

He socializes with people who please him.

He eats the food that brings him joy and wears the clothes that adorn him beautifully.

When he hears of new luxuries he experiments with them.

In this brief life he is committed to having the enjoyment, the peace, the fun and the excitement that he desires.

There is no one around to tell him when to stop or to take just enough.

And because the Entrepreneur wants to live a long, happy and healthy indulgent life he is always well aware of his responsibility for his actions.

The Entrepreneur, wise in years, knows how best to blend indulgence and discipline.

His goal is to burn brightly and long.

18-The Entrepreneur embraces rapid change

The Entrepreneur understands that when many things change simultaneously it is a rare opportunity.

As multiple doors close forever and entries into new ones beckon - the Entrepreneur is excited.

This is the chance – and the opportunity – that he has been working toward.

The old ways of doing things are now behind him. Though he feels naked and yes slightly unsettled, he looks toward the open doors and moves energetically toward them.

He will take a moment to feel the sun and the air on his naked body.

It is a reminder of how he came into the world - and how he will leave it.

Therefore he moves toward the open door.

He reminds himself that he is ready and eager to have the things he said he always wanted.

The Entrepreneur understands that rapid change – when some things die and some things bloom means that what he is doing is working.

The Entrepreneur moves forward and doesn't look back.

19-The Entrepreneur knows money buys happiness

Does money buy happiness?

It's questions like this that give the Entrepreneur a chuckle during the course of a typically brutal day.

Money is the source of all comfort and freedom from strain in life – if you have a lot of it, you have more comfort, more freedom, more time and most important, more space between you and other scrabbling humans fighting for survival.

The only people who have the time or inclination to consider such an absurd idea are ones whose lives are not marked by struggle – namely, tenured professors or subsidized social scientists.

When such people investigate this kind of problem, what they are doing is missing the real question – why can't people learn how to use their freedom?

If he is ever drawn into the question of whether or not money buys happiness the Entrepreneur will make a joke of it by saying, "Maybe not, but I sure as hell know poverty causes mental illness."

And because the Entrepreneur does not want to devolve into a drooling, muttering homeless person, he will brush past this ridiculous question and keep right on keeping on toward his goals of making as much money for as little effort as possible.

20-The Entrepreneur relishes his victories

When the Entrepreneur wins, he smiles.

He may think, I maneuvered or acted ingeniously to achieve my aim.

He knows he was focused and pushed through to the end. He achieved something for himself that only he could do.

He exhales and sits back. He is content with winning.

The Entrepreneur is happy because he has made a mere thought into something real. He enjoys the moment because this is what it's all about.

He may remember the struggle and how impossible it seemed. This makes him even happier and widens his smile.

This moment of celebration makes him even more determined to attack the next thing on his list. He is flush with the feeling of being alive.

The Entrepreneur enjoys what he has become as a result of this victory. He views it in context - as just another victory in a long line that he has made.

He feels the sunshine on his face and is certain of future success.

21-The Entrepreneur understands the stakes

The Entrepreneur notices the consequences of failure all around him.

Millions have given up on life itself and die in the gutter.

Millions more have quietly surrendered and are the real walking dead.

The majority don't even understand what's at stake and waste their one and only life.

The Entrepreneur is on point at all times.

He cannot fail.

To fail would mean he didn't do everything in his power to succeed.

It would mean he would endure a double failure – to his outward goal and himself.

Every day he works to the best of his capacity. He is content he is fulfilling his promise to himself.

He knows the outward success will come.

The alternative is too horrible to consider - poverty, misery and an early death.

The Entrepreneur knows these are the true stakes and he is playing to win.

22-The Entrepreneur understands this business formula

The goal of business is to make money.

The Entrepreneur's business goal is to make as much money with as little effort and risk as possible.

From a system's standpoint, this is the only logical conclusion.

With money as the goal of the process, the next step is to minimize the inputs.

Those inputs are defined as "work" and "risk."

If you are measuring your results as money, what value does "work" add?

Does it make you feel good that you expended effort into a "worthwhile" project?

That may be a useless emotion – inherited from the Puritan work ethic, or some notion of being a good member of society.

In other words, it's pointless. Once you have the money you won't care about what you did to get it.

And more to the point you won't care about what other people think about how you got it. They will think what they will think.

And most of them will still be poor and you will be rich.

As far as risk is concerned, this is another emotional component that doesn't have a place in a logical construct.

Some people like the gambler's high that comes with risk, and most gambler's wind up either losing or giving their winnings back to the house.

Why risk when you don't have to?

You want a sure thing, or the ability to gamble with other people's money in order to achieve your output, which is money.

So again, the Entrepreneur's business model is to make as much money with as little effort and risk as possible.

For the Entrepreneur in a hurry, you want to add, "as fast as possible."

Because again, there's no value in taking a long time to get the output – except some old fashioned notion that you have to prove something to someone over whether or not you deserve the money.

The goal of business is to make money.

The Entrepreneur's business goal is to make it now, with little work and no risk.

23-The Entrepreneur maintains clarity

The Entrepreneur has awakened.

He is aware at all times that this is his one and only life to do with as he wishes.

He rests within himself and lets the world spin.

The Entrepreneur uses his mind to achieve the aims he has set for himself.

One of these is to have a clear mind.

If shadows attempt to creep in, he casts a light on them.

If doubt begins to take hold he reminds himself that he is the director and not a slave.

He breathes easily, content with the simple life he has created - one that is centered on his own happiness and comfort.

This simple practice has become a habit that keeps his thoughts even at all times.

The Entrepreneur uses his clear mind to remain focused on himself.

He know this feedback loop - from awakening, to decision to focus - atop simple breathing - helps him achieve both his material and emotional objectives.

The Entrepreneur begins and ends every day with a clear mind.

It is his greatest resource and the source of all his wealth.

24-The Entrepreneur knows life is about survival of the fittest

The Entrepreneur knows this basic law of nature cannot be avoided.

The strong will live and the weak will die.

Even in societies where there are "safety nets" put into place, there are winners and losers.

In some advanced systems, different kinds of winners emerge – those skilled more in cunning than physical prowess, but the truth remains – every human being has to fight simply for the right to survive, never mind grab a share of the spoils.

The Entrepreneur assesses the strengths necessary to thrive in his current circumstances.

He avoids the traps that lure the weak into self-destruction – such as food and drink which are thousands of years old.

He also notes the modern traps – excessive media, bogus organizations and financial contracts that are meant to exploit those who don't think for themselves.

He works on his most precious survival muscle – his mind – to find the opportunities necessary to rise above those who are suffering.

The Entrepreneur attends to his own survival above all else, ensuring that he lives the long and happy life he has decided to give to himself.

25-The Entrepreneur believes in his own cause

When the Entrepreneur listens to someone explain to him why he has to believe in some vague goal he looks at them as if they escaped from a mental institution.

The cause has nothing to do with him. It appears to have sprung from out of nowhere.

The Entrepreneur knows that quite often the entire thing has been manufactured by an advocacy organization, politician or corporation.

There is a bit of entertainment value in these interactions.

The Entrepreneur is intrigued by how somebody can have their mind hijacked by something that does not benefit or harm them directly.

But then the Entrepreneur gets back to his own business. Which is his own cause.

The Entrepreneur is more enthusiastic about this cause than he is about anything floating out there in the ether.

He believes that his cause is right and just.

He knows that his cause will deliver astounding benefits.

He knows his cause is a matter of life and death.

The Entrepreneur's cause is simple – to maximize his good and minimize his pain.

That is the only rational thing he can ever care about.

And while he is busy with his own sacred mission he is sometimes grateful that other people with their frivolous movements are too busy to bother him.

26-The Entrepreneur knows how easy it is to fall asleep

While some Entrepreneurs are born, most are self-made.

That is, they wake up to reality.

They may have been abandoned as children and realized that they are the only ones who will secure their safety and security.

Or they may have gotten to middle-age and realized how much of what they're doing is a pre-programmed charade.

Having once woken up, the self-made Entrepreneur knows he must stay on alert.

It's so easy to fall back asleep.

It's so easy to coast along and take part in shallow delights.

It's so easy to not do the things that need to be done.

It's easy to give up.

The self-made Entrepreneur remind himself daily that he is the authority over his own life.

That he is the one responsible for whether he succeeds or fails.

The self-made Entrepreneur remains awake at all times – because he knows the alternative is to return to a trance-like state marked by neither true happiness nor fulfillment.

27-The Entrepreneur acts when others hesitate

The Entrepreneur has a bias for action at all times, and especially when others are timid.

If he sees fear or inertia - inaction for no factual reason, the Entrepreneur takes bold action.

He does so because when others are timid a bold stroke mesmerizes them.

He does so because he fills a vacuum left by other's inaction.

The Entrepreneur takes bold action when others hesitate because it is an opening that is fleeting and will get him much further than during times when others are humming along.

He knows inaction is marked by people looking around waiting for something to happen. The Entrepreneur is happy to oblige.

The Entrepreneur reaps a multiple of his action and extends his legend by proving he is courageous while others are afraid.

28-The Entrepreneur walks through the open door

Once the Entrepreneur establishes his authority, he begins looking for opportunity.

The Entrepreneur has decided he wants more - a better, easier life - and this comes through a better opportunity.

As the Entrepreneur ceases to care about things that do not affect him, opportunities are easier to spot.

As the Entrepreneur fully appreciates how much of what he thought was his to have (or allowed) was actually programmed into him by false prophets, opportunities are easier to create.

With all these obstacles removed and his healthy sense of self-regard, the Entrepreneur knows finding a new opportunity is as easy as walking through an open door.

He knows what he wants to find on the opposite side of that door and that there is an easy way to get there.

He keeps his mind clear and is always ready.

The door is available to him and today may be the day he walks through it into the life he has decided he wants for himself.

29-The Entrepreneur creates a new reality

By believing in his mission and dedicating himself to

it without reservation, the Entrepreneur creates something that never existed.

It is his own reality that is conjured up in his mind.

By taking focused effort he brings it into the world in such a way that others come across it and it appears to them as if it always existed.

Some accomplish this through sneaky means or simple fraud.

The Entrepreneur knows, however, that the sturdiest way to create his reality is by doing so without guile.

That is, he states that this is the truth in a steady and confident manner.

Because it is true in his mind and he has stated in a matter-of-fact manner, he is not questioned.

He knows how many people he needs for it to become self-sustaining in the outside world.

And because he has created it in such a way that it is bed rock solid he can be patient so that it becomes so – because it is so first in his mind.

30-The Entrepreneur knows people only want good news

When someone asks, 'how was your weekend,' the Entrepreneur replies with something pleasant.

The Entrepreneur understands other's opinion of him is based on the news he broadcasts.

Therefore everything is always good and life is proceeding as expected.

The Entrepreneur keeps his troubles secret and works to fix them without looking for sympathy.

Letting other people know your troubles lowers their opinion of you and can make your situation worse. (Because the Entrepreneur knows kicking someone when they are down is a venerable tradition.)

The Entrepreneur projects an optimistic outlook at all times. It increases others' estimation of him and increases his power. If it lifts others up, so be it.

It allows him to carry on with his plan where the news is always good because it is of his own design.

31-The Entrepreneur doesn't try

The Entrepreneur simply does the thing he sets out to do. He doesn't hope, pray or beg.

The Entrepreneur doesn't strain or cry out in anguish.

He simply does the thing he set out to do.

The Entrepreneur doesn't consult books, websites, or psychics.

He simply sets out to do the thing he said he would do.

The Entrepreneur can do this because he first spent the most valuable effort in preparing his mind.

He has taken the time to reclaim his authority over his own life.

He believes deep in his bones that he deserves every good thing he decides to have.

And after this preliminary work is complete, he formulated a goal that will achieve his aims.

And because the Entrepreneur is the ruler of his life and has laid claim to every good thing his goal proceeds smoothly.

The deed is done before he begins.

And while he may expend effort and even sweat or long hours and great risk he never tries.

He simply does the thing he set out to do.

32-The Entrepreneurs is always selling

The Entrepreneur knows people want to be sold.

It doesn't even matter what – people have been conditioned to behave as if buying is proof they are alive.

Therefore the Entrepreneur sells what makes people feel alive.

He shows optimism and the promise of a better

tomorrow.

He sells safety and the guarantee of security.

The Entrepreneur has fun selling because it is a joyous act – two parties coming together to exchange cash for goods or services – where both get something from the transaction.

Sales is one of the few positive direct interactions between human beings and the Entrepreneur follows this simple idea.

The Entrepreneurs sells and brightens the lives of his customers and this is how he gets customers for life.

And because it is joyous, and what people want to do, the Entrepreneur is always selling – it is one of his defining characteristics, because it is also a sign of life, a spark of action and creativity.

The Entrepreneur embodies all of this – necessity, joy, energy and creativity – and thus manufactures an aura about him that is dynamic and attracts more money to his cause.

33-The Entrepreneur can play a role

Because he observes and knows the rules of situations, the Entrepreneur adopts the conventions required.

He does what is necessary to achieve competence – that alone will secure his position.

And the Entrepreneur will do a little more – just enough so that he garners respect without drawing too much attention.

If excellence will be rewarded with promotion or money then he will deliver excellence.

But if he is in a waystation he maintains the status quo.

The Entrepreneur will then use his surplus energy to plan and execute the next stage in his quest.

But the Entrepreneur does not rebel to make a noise. Nor does he shirk his duties in resentment.

The Entrepreneur is always about maximizing benefit from his situation with his eye on the long-term goal.

And so whatever role he is given at the moment he will fulfill as determined by conditions.

But his goal remains - to serve his own cause, have the things he desires and minimize annoyances.

Ultimately the Entrepreneur will achieve the independence that is his primary purpose.

34-The Entrepreneur knows success is the best revenge

When he is bouncing back or dusting himself off, the Entrepreneur focuses on revenge.

His focus is on the best kind of revenge – which is showing up like a star, winning at everything he does, ignoring any scars or voices that make a lesser man doubt himself.

The Entrepreneur knows that success is manufactured in the mind and he relegates failure and embarrassment into a data file to use to refine his approach and for no other purpose.

The Entrepreneur knows that assuming success - especially after a failure - confounds his opposition and makes them doubt themselves.

But he doesn't even care about this - because true success in a vengeful fashion means acting as if your enemies do not exist.

So the Entrepreneur's true aim remains his success. Everything else can become part of his legend – including the consternation of his enemies.

And because this concept is good for a laugh, he gets right back to the game.

This good cheer is enough to erase any lingering pain and make the way ahead fun and full of light.

35-The Entrepreneur lets other people have their morality

The Entrepreneur is not swayed by the moral arguments of others.

There are some points he may agree with and some that he does not even consider. But he lives his own morality from within.

He does not allow others to hijack his actions and the pursuit of his goal merely because they disapprove. And that really is the heart of a lot of disapproval – is people making a moral judgment about you.

Because the Entrepreneur rests within himself and his own moral code he ignores the preachers and naysayers.

In this matter he sees morality as it really is – a means of control that others attempt to use to restrict his actions.

And because the core of his moral code is doing what he thinks is best for himself he will not have it.

The Entrepreneur is content to go about his business. If other people have chosen to wriggle around like a fish on the hook of their own morality that is their choice.

And as himself, they will have to face the consequences of those choices.

36-The Entrepreneur cultivates his energy

The Entrepreneur knows it takes energy to accomplish his worthwhile goals. He may also have other obligations that require energy as well.

Not content to throw everything away - after all, what he wants is everything - the Entrepreneur becomes shrewd with his effort.

He puts his best energy into the goal that will deliver the biggest result.

If he has a job that barely pays the bills and a business idea that will make him rich, he will shift into maintenance mode at work to pay for the business.

The Entrepreneur has obviously cut out distractions that keep people poor, such as media, overeating and gossip, so he has gained energy from that self-audit.

He also does something counter-intuitive - putting more energy into family and physical fitness - because these areas pay more than they cost. When he loves his family and close friends, and his body, he has more energy for the big project.

All along, he remains shrewd - conserving where it makes most sense, eliminating where it's obvious and paying into activities that reward him with the energy he needs for the big score.

The Entrepreneur knows one way to look at how he has lived his life, post-transformation, is to look at where he chose to spend his time and energy in the pursuit of his new ideal.

37-What is the Entrepreneur's project?

The Entrepreneur's project is his own life.

That he first understands his own unlimited authority over his life.

That he is the owner of his person.

That he has the innate right to use his life as he pleases.

That he has the power to decide what he believes and how he speaks and acts.

That he can do as he decides, can enjoy the pleasures and avoid the pain that he has identified.

The Entrepreneur's project is limited only by his imagination and his ability to understand and put his power into practice.

That the scope of his project is limited only by his ability to enjoy the life he has for his own sake, to use it as he wishes and have not a care for the ideas and morals of others that would prevent him from doing any of the above.

Therefore the Entrepreneur's project is not only to claim and use his authority but also to remove the limits he encounters that keep the scope of his project smaller than it needs to be.

38-The Entrepreneur does not go to an empty well

When the Entrepreneur is in the hunt for money he does not try to get it from those who do not have it.

He does not try to get paid more than an industry or company pays.

You can't make $30 an hour working at Burger King.

Yes, with financing you can sell hot tubs to the poor.

But unless he has control over the financing vehicle he is always fighting the wind.

The Entrepreneur plants himself in the middle of a whirlwind of free cash.

He enjoys the weather and puts as much in his pocket as he can.

He charges more than his competitors in this environment.

When money is abundant the Entrepreneur knows there is always a thirst for more and unique.

He understands that when money is flowing people let their guard down.

He also understands that when money is not flowing it is held onto with an iron fist and beady eyes.

The Entrepreneur understands the reality and psychology of money and stays in the realm of milk and honey - always offering more and better than those around him.

39-The Entrepreneur wants everyone to be an Entrepreneur

The Entrepreneur knows when everyone is awake and

attuned to their own self-interest it will lead to less violence, less strife and more productivity – and more happiness.

The Entrepreneur understands that misery comes from enslavement. When millions and even billions bow down in worship to mere mortals that is when problems begin

That is how wars start. That is how revolutions and inner-city violence fester and burst into the open.

On the other hand when everyone is an Entrepreneur, when everyone understands that they are responsible for their own well-being, a peace will come over the world that has never existed.

These new Entrepreneurs will cease to be slaves and will tumble the thieving masters without ever firing a shot. They will look around and realize they have every right to every good thing and they will make it so.

The Entrepreneur wants others to wake up so that he has more equals with which to play, conspire and enjoy life with.

40-The Entrepreneur is wary of fame

For the Entrepreneur, fame is a thing.

He treats it as a tool and an asset and never confuses it with his real self. He may wield it as a disguise or a weapon, but it is nothing more than a suit of clothes.

He understands fame is a drug for the masses and it can help him acquire the things and experiences he wants with less effort than it takes a normal person.

In many cases there are things you can never acquire without fame.

Thus the Entrepreneur sees it for what it is - a force multiplier for his aims - useful and profitable but never is it himself.

He never pursues it for its own sake but for the purpose of fulfilling his aims.

This posture allows him to avoid the pitfalls of fame that include delusion, mental illness and a degenerate character.

41-The Entrepreneur keeps his life simple

The Entrepreneur is focused on maximizing his enjoyment and reducing his pain.

He knows his enjoyment comes with a price tag. That is why he's always focused on money.

And because making money is a primary human activity he finds great enjoyment in its pursuit. Also because making money reduces the pains he has to endure.

But the simplicity of his life comes from not doing things that are of no value – media consumption, hobbies and diversions are for those who are content to glide. They're not primary activities but childlike past times.

He does enjoy the company of others but only those who are also engaged and leading productive lives. Otherwise he's forced to listen to complaints and excuses which are nothing but pain to him.

In other words the Entrepreneur is about his business – his purpose – and leaves the concerns of others alone.

42-The Entrepreneur controls his time

The Entrepreneur makes time for what he wants to do no matter his other concerns.

He cannot comprehend a lack of time as an excuse.

If he has a job and a family and decides he needs to start a business or pursue a goal in addition, he figures out a way.

The Entrepreneur disciplines himself to take care of obligations so that time is available.

He begins his day with the thing he wants to do - a simple trick that gives him more energy to attend to the mundane, and makes ordinary life feel more like a joy than a burden.

The Entrepreneur sets deadlines for himself and meets them.

He tracks his progress to see if there is a way to become more time efficient. And he does most of this in his head.

His mind is the ultimate computer and he trains himself to be aware of time and doesn't let it slip or dissolve into the past.

The Entrepreneur is a master of time because that is how his life is recorded. And he aims to make the most of what he has.

43-The Entrepreneur seeks to become a master

The Entrepreneur's goal is for these principles to operate in the background.

He strives to live without thinking of these ideas or having to reference them like a Bible.

He sees minor players exalting the virtues of the laws of power as if they are an end in themselves. They are not. Power is an end in itself.

The Entrepreneur understands that to truly enjoy the fruits of power is to be able to live without thinking, speaking or writing about these ideas. They become second nature, distilled into the fiber of his being.

The Entrepreneur simply becomes an avatar of these principles and need not say a word regarding the source of his knowledge.

To achieve this state he will study them in private until such time his life has become a reflection of rational self-interest – when his actions and results are in harmony and his life is filled with prosperity and peace of mind.

44-The Entrepreneur is in one business

The Entrepreneur is only in the business of himself.

The wellbeing of his one and only business is his only concern.

He is aware of costs and revenue at all times. He works to minimize disruption and maximize benefit.

He puts the tending of his business first - before he thinks about looking to the left or right at the affairs of others.

His best day is when he doesn't pay attention to them at all.

He makes his own business his dwelling and luxuriates within it.

His preference is to never go outside of his own gate.

He is happy with himself because he knows he is his own best ally.

He consults his own priorities before seeking the counsel of others.

He weighs associations against the needs of his business.

He calculates potential profit against risk and effort and costs required.

He lives easily with singular focus.

He is cheerful because he is secure.

He shares his bounty with himself first and if there is surplus he considers carefully where to invest it, starting with his family and the community that supports him.

45-The Entrepreneur uses this 3-stage antidote for frustration

When the Entrepreneur experiences frustration he takes responsibility.

He may have been cheated out of ignorance or weakness.

To regain the advantage he takes responsibility for his part in the matter.

But most of all he takes responsibility for fixing the situation.

The Entrepreneur then takes action to solve his frustration.

He may have to fight to recover a loss or simply take a new direction to get what he wants.

And the more action he takes to create the result he wants, the less he feels frustrated.

All that's left is the lesson over how the negative result occurred - and a resolve to never let it happen again.

The Entrepreneur reviews these 3 stages -

responsibility, action and resolve - and makes them a part of his being.

Over time he is grateful for the control this experience and response has provided to him.

46-The Entrepreneur always takes another step

When he is working, the Entrepreneur always takes another step further than he thought he could go.

No matter what he imagined was possible, he knows it is just a construct and determines to push his self-imposed limit.

This discipline serves him well. Over time he has proven to himself that he can do what others think is impossible.

This discipline builds his self-regard in addition to his results.

The Entrepreneur has learned to trust his own effort because he never stops.
He knows there are times when he has to draw on the reserves he has built up. For the most part he enjoys his strength.

The Entrepreneur also enjoys the fruit of his effort - more results, natural confidence and the knowledge that he can handle any challenge.

Knowing all this in advance, when the question of

whether or not he can take another step arises in his mind, he laughs and is already walking before he needs to answer it.

47-The Entrepreneur uses anger

It is understandable for a newborn Entrepreneur to be angry.

He has woken up to reality and realized that he has not looked after his own self-interest for most of his life.

He has done what he has been told, he has done what he thought was right, he has followed bad advice – and is in a worse position then he ought to be.

Once awakened, this new Entrepreneur realizes how he has been robbed. This can cause an angry state.

However there is a way to break through from simple anger to using it as a tool.

The newborn Entrepreneur must redirect his anger toward his condition – while taking responsibility for creating his circumstances.

He is in a place he wants to leave. He will use this anger as fuel.

He will draw on the idea that he should have more, be more and experience greater freedom.

He will use this anger to launch himself to where he is

supposed to be.

At that point the anger will be gone. He has freed himself from the trap of his own making. He is wise enough not to do it again.

And he has broken into the open field where he lives free and calm and happy knowing he has taken care of his own interests first

This will prevent anger from ever rising again.

48-The Entrepreneur never fights the tape

If business sentiment and consumer dollars are going in a certain direction the Entrepreneur maximizes his take off this phenomenon.

And he understands it as such – a phenomenon that will last a certain amount of time.

As such he knows it is larger than any individual and certainly resistant to logic or caution. If money is flowing into an investment - even if it makes no sense - he can profit.

If people want to buy billions of dollar worth of energy drinks that look like radioactive goo, he will sell it if he can.

At the same time he will research business opportunities for renal failure clinics because that will be an outcome of consuming something so bad for you.

The point is the Entrepreneur doesn't need to believe or even like what is happening in the marketplace.

He sees it and capitalizes on it and then he sleeps soundly.

And he is always looking for where the herd is going, because that is the reality of the marketplace and has been so for thousands of years.

49-The Entrepreneur knows identity is stronger than desire

The Entrepreneur observes how most people will hold on to their identity rather than do the things necessary to get the results they say they desire.

The concept of identity comes from beliefs, family group, nationality and so on.

People would rather cling to these deep-rooted concepts than step into the light and live a better life.

The Entrepreneur knows he is not above this primitive impulse.

Therefore, he searches his own self-concept and roots out all ingrained ideas about who and what he is supposed to be.

At the conscious level he has decided who he is and what he wants and he works toward it.

At the same time he knows that he is susceptible to

normal human weakness.

He is ruthless when doubt creeps in. He knows this is a tactic of self-concept to keep him in his place.

But because he has decided that his place is where he chooses, he remains vigilant against self-sabotage.

The Entrepreneur knows creating his own identity is one of his most important tasks and his crowning achievement.

50-The Entrepreneur rests when he is weary

After a great effort, the Entrepreneur takes a rest.

He knows it is not the time to try something new - his energy and more important, decision making, are off.

He cares for his body and his mind, knowing they are the vehicles by which he accomplishes great things.

He will take the time to observe, and to plan. He will consider what is going right. He will look for the missing piece, or what can be improved.

He will ask himself what is next to be done when his energy is restored.

The Entrepreneur takes time to enjoy the results of his effort and build his self-regard - that he does great things with his will and his body and that rest is part of his plan.

He knows this is a great interlude for leaps of

imagination and problem solving - that as a human being everything moves in cycles and he is wise enough to wait until he is ready for a new assault on a goal he has been considering.

The Entrepreneur's time of rest can sometimes be even more productive than times of effort - because this is when research is conducted and strategies are made.

For the Entrepreneur, times of rest are enjoyable and germinate the seeds of greater accomplishment.

51-The Entrepreneur can smile when he's getting screwed

There are times when a negotiation doesn't go the Entrepreneur's way.

When it becomes clear he's getting screwed, he smiles, and says, "great!"

This while his mind is working at how to recoup the loss or get a better deal some other way.

It's not a matter of taking one for the team or forgiveness or some silly notion.

It's about getting what he needs as fast as he can get it.

Fighting with folks who just put the screws to him can only impede his progress.

Besides, he just got a stark reminder that everyone else is looking out for their own self-interest just as much as he is – or should be. (He knows he should have seen it coming.)

So he means it when he says great because that just gave him an even better reason to go and do something he's been wanting to do.

And that's super!

52-The Entrepreneur will share when others are ready

The Entrepreneur mostly keeps his way to himself.

He is busy with his project - and most would abuse him for his beliefs.

But when he sees someone lost or bewildered - and ready to listen, he will share his story.

He will let the other know that they are lost because they are following bad directions.

He will demonstrate how they are unhappy because they believe in the wrong ideals.

He will prove how living for yourself is a way out of depression and hopelessness.

He will challenge them to prove the mirages promised by others are real.

The Entrepreneur, in his calm and measured way, will help them take their first steps to freedom.

He will delight in the look of awareness on their faces to their new reality.

Then he will leave them to their own devices, armed with the principles of authority, reason and action.

53-The Entrepreneur asks himself this question

What is the best use of my mental energy?

The Entrepreneur asks himself this question when planning his long term strategy and every day as he begins.

He is vigilant against distraction – indeed, he views it as a thief that would steal his most precious resource.

The Entrepreneur applies his mental faculty to the thing he loves most – himself and his aim.

This is where he is happy, and he feeds off the energy created from the making of his own life.

Every moment spent working on his own possession is proof that he has no other obligation, that there is no better use of his life than his own.

His mind and body are refreshed from this perpetual loop and he has the energy to work and enjoy the fruit of his labor.

The Entrepreneur has full use of his imagination because his mind is unconcerned with the care of the world.

He has reduced the noise to a white din through which he moves with grace. He sees other struggle and moves on past.

His mind is clear and focused on his goal.

Every day is a celebration of his existence that receives his full attention. He luxuriates in his oasis and respects himself by strengthening and building his creation.

All this by paying attention to his own needs, using his full authority and using his mind to direct his action.

54-The Entrepreneur knows most are stuck in permanent childhood

The Entrepreneur knows he is dealing with a grade school mentality when he interacts with people on a daily basis. He doesn't look at their dress or other appearances, but focuses on behavior.

When he sees people buying toys they can't afford, spending hours in front of screens, he sees people who are acting like children – content to believe the world is a magical place and it is okay to while away the hours entertaining themselves.

When he sees people avoiding work, or chattering about others, he sees children. When he sees the equivalent of playground bullying in the workplace, or favoritism or avoiding responsibility, he sees the child's mind in play.

And when he sees people whining about life being unfair, or waiting for someone to come to their rescue, he sees a child.

As with other behaviors, this is a double-edged sword to the Entrepreneur.

On the annoying side, it is something that has to be accommodated and managed.

On the plus side children can be manipulated – in fact they love it as long as their fantasy remains unperturbed.

They can be threatened, bullied, punished, put in time-out and set against each other – the Entrepreneur knows all this can be used to his advantage, as long as he maintains the veneer of treating others as adults with valued opinions while calculating how to treat them as children internally.

55-The Entrepreneur sets his own standard

The Entrepreneur has created the image of his ideal life.

He has taken authority over his own life and accepts that all power and responsibility are his.

Then he sets forth to do the things necessary to fulfill his mission.

He starts with an idea of what he can accomplish.

Then he does the thing - tracking what works and what doesn't.

Very quickly he has a baseline.

Then the Entrepreneur works to double his effectiveness.

He continues tracking his results - and works to double again.

The Entrepreneur sets his own standard because he is the only reliable source of what is possible.

Because his goals are his own, as is his authority and action, he is simply doing what is necessary to make his life whole.

He may know how impossible it looks to others but doesn't care.

The Entrepreneur is only concerned about how he feels when his head hits the pillow at night.

Was he true to himself?

56-The Entrepreneur is self-reliant

Of course the Entrepreneur knows all results are up to him to create.

And there is another kind of self-reliance he also

cultivates:

Belief in his own ideas.

The Entrepreneur trusts his judgment, and his calculated instinct when he has an idea for a project.

He knows that if the basis is sound, all he has to do is see it through.

The Entrepreneur may have already felt the sting of watching his idea grow and succeed under someone else's guidance.

If not, he is aware of the stories of those who could have succeeded – if they had only followed through.

The Entrepreneur knows this type of self-reliance can also be called courage, or conviction.

He takes a moment, when working on an infant idea, to recognize he is in the crucible between realizing his goal and simply being a quitter.

The courage to see an idea through, from glimmer to sketch to model and success is the essence of what he has decided to do with his power.

The Entrepreneur's self-reliance is what makes him into the man he wants to be.

And not just a success – but someone who made a reality out of nothing but his breath and his brain.

57-The Entrepreneur knows men are born in battle

The Entrepreneur will spend time cultivating his authority.

Thinking about his sovereignty over his own affairs – and the capacity for action.

But there comes a time when he knows he must step onto the field.

No man was ever born contemplating his plans.

Worse, there are men who have died who have never been born.

The Entrepreneur knows he will only become himself when he enters the fray – and takes the first blow.

He knows he will have to defend himself, and strike out at his adversaries.

The Entrepreneur seeks to baptize himself in the arena – of business, sport and love.

He considers the first step – and is prepared to be changed by the conflict.

In the midst of battle, he renews his cause – and rallies himself to fight to the other side.

He is already changing, already becoming different than the boy who dreamed of greatness.

As his shell toughens and his muscles heave, his mind bursts into life.

He discovers new strength, new reserves of energy.

Each skirmish strengthens his drive to reach the other side of the field.

He sees the bloody banner waving in the distance and knows it is his to own.

The Entrepreneur launches himself into battle, knowing it will make him the man he has envisioned himself to be.

58-The Entrepreneur knows people already live in augmented reality

Modern humans have been raised in constant immersion in media. First televised and now digital, this media has become an intertwined strand of their perception of reality.

So for most people the concept of reality is partially based on and driven by things that do not exist.

This includes everything from their plans and conversations to events and facts.

This leaves people vulnerable to pure reality when it strikes.

It wakes them up and terrifies them.

Then they will run to the shelter of the next available ameliorative fantasy.

For the Entrepreneur this is a potent understanding of the modern human psyche.

Therefore the Entrepreneur's first task is to ensure his mind is always rooted in reality.

His next task is to make use of the part-automatons he encounters on a daily basis. He doesn't want to do too much to disturb them from their slumber for fear of encountering their wrath.

But he does make use of their pliability – for his commercial aims and to gain what he wants.

For the most part he lets them sleep and tiptoes along his path of his fabulous, real life.

59-The Entrepreneur capitalizes on the errors of his adversaries

When engaged in commerce the Entrepreneur makes the most of his opponent's mistakes.

In some cases when the error is made the advantage tilts to him by default.

He doesn't have to crow about it, just lets it lie there and accepts the concession that results on the back of their mistake.

Other times he will have to point out what they either don't see or don't want to acknowledge.

There will be times he has to go in for the kill and make it clear that their incompetence is reason to let him have the field.

Overall the Entrepreneur's competence will give him this advantage over and over again.

So he has learned to wait for it – especially when the competitor is a loud mouth.

In other words, clods often trip over their own incompetence.

Because of this awareness, the Entrepreneur also ensures that he appears gracious in victory.

(He knew they would fail and simply fixes the mistake while taking his share.)

This way he wins twice – in prize and reputation.

60-The Entrepreneur is mentally tough

The Entrepreneur lives with the premise that life is tough.

There are as many challenges as there are rewards.

Further, the challenges are the path to rewards.

So when life happens the Entrepreneur handles it.

When he encounters "problems" that derail others he takes care of them as a matter of fact.

He saves his energy for playing offense.

Getting in front of and keeping problems from occurring is a better use of his energy.

So that when true challenges arise he has the resources and capacity to engage them.

The Entrepreneur uses the examples of success and failure all around him as his guide to navigating the actual conditions of life.

61-The Entrepreneur knows man is god on earth

The Entrepreneur does not concern himself with the question of whether or not there is a God in the sky – his concern is to prosper on Earth.

By looking around him, and even with a little bit of history, he quickly comes to see that Man rules over the Earth – that no divine being has ever interceded in the affairs of humanity.

Therefore the idea of a ghost swooping down to help him, or prevent him from harming another, does not ever enter his equation.

He is only concerned with living on this planet, and therefore does understand he has to learn the ways of

Man – which include paying lip service to false gods and morality systems that the Entrepreneur understands are merely systems of controlling large populations, in the same way the Invisible Fence can keep your dog on the property.

62-The Entrepreneur understands the folly of working for money

The Entrepreneur understands that labor is in excess supply, and therefore wages will always be suppressed.

Therefore, an individual can never earn enough from straight labor to ever cease his labors.

From the outset, this strikes the Entrepreneur as a bad deal. Why would anyone work in order to support themselves, knowing they will never be paid enough?

He also understands that most people, driven by the primitive survival portion of their brains, never take the time to think their way out of this conundrum. After all, billions of people work, so it must be right – right?

Wrong.

The Entrepreneur born into poverty takes a quick look around him and realizes that every one of his poor relations that goes to work every day, bitching and complaining the whole time, simply don't have the courage or the creativity to figure out a better way.

He understands quickly that if he is not willing to

outright steal the resources necessary to live a life of ease and enjoyment, then he had better get busy making money off the labor of lots of other people.

There are many ways to do this, but the main idea is that exchanging a single unit of time for a single unit of currency is a losing proposition – and that the Entrepreneur is always thinking of how to exploit the labor of others.

63-The Entrepreneur cultivates confidence

Confidence is the cornerstone of the Entrepreneur's personality – he sees the world differently than others, and understands his place is wherever he chooses to be.

He knows people want to be led in words and deeds and will abdicate their self-control in the presence of someone who appears to know what they are doing.

If he is in the world without status or capital, he makes cultivating confidence his number one priority – it is the one tool free to all that can be used to acquire the rest.

And he understands the impact of confidence on others – the ones he knows to be afraid and unsure of themselves.

He is unselfish in sharing his confidence with others around him, because he knows they will feed upon it like plants to the sun.

The Entrepreneur also knows that a mass of followers

will make him appear confident to those he has never met, enabling him to become a self-fulfilling prophecy.

64-The Entrepreneur knows gang activity when he sees it

When firefighters show up at a city council meeting in uniform to make a case for higher rates of pay, more lavish perks and cost-free retirement packages, the Entrepreneur sees gang activity.

When the elderly band together to lobby government for free medical care at the expense of those still in the workforce, the Entrepreneur sees a gang.

The Entrepreneur defines gang activity as any small group that uses intimidation, force of numbers and disruptive threats to extract more benefit from the system than they have contributed.

And he sees it everywhere – while modern gangs wear socially acceptable disguises that convey normality, he sees barbarians forcing their way to the table with the threat of chaos if their demands are not met.

The Entrepreneur may elect to join a gang, or ally himself with one, but he never loses sight of the fact that small dedicated groups of marauders have always banded together to demand tribute.

65-The Entrepreneur worships no heroes

The Entrepreneur views celebrity worship as a two-stage proxy for the meek.

It provides the worshippers with an outlet for a rich fantasy life, and if they engage in gazing at the other for long enough, they are rendered too weak to reach out and grab some of that glamour for themselves.

So yes, they are the modern pantheon of minor deities who engage in adventures for others to enjoy vicariously and they serve to instruct via example.

The Entrepreneur does not engage in hero worship, celebrity or otherwise.

It is a matter of not giving away his power and not wasting time and energy.

If he seeks to install himself as an object of worship, that is understandable, as it is a proven method for acquiring goods and ease.

The Entrepreneur worships only himself.

66-The Entrepreneur understands the consequences of failure

The Entrepreneur understands there are no do-overs, second chances -- or even prizes for second place.

Everything is all or nothing.

To think otherwise is to live within a worldview that does not take into account the reality of time and mortality.

When working on an opportunity, the Entrepreneur will do anything to win -- there is no telling if this is the best chance he has to make a fortune, or acquire the gains he desires.

Losing money, or a deal, could take years to repair -- and the loss to confidence and status may be permanent.

For many things in life there are no second chances, ever.

The Entrepreneur is both fearful and enraged by the possibility of failure. Of course it is always possible, and this drives him like a dark specter.

The idea that he could be thwarted by another enrages him, and sharpens his drive.

There are people who want to see him fail, and who will enjoy the sight of his suffering.

The consequences of failure are always present in the mind of the Entrepreneur – he understands that true success means getting the results you are after, and that to be comforted by the prospect of a safety net is almost worse than never leaving the ledge.

67-The Entrepreneur knows he will be dead for a million years

The Entrepreneur understands he is mortal and does

not expect his consciousness to survive the death of his body.

He also understands that he will not be missed, the same way a drop of water can be subtracted from the ocean without a trace of memory.

For the Entrepreneur, death is not just final but a matter of perspective – an 80 year life in the face of a million year void lends greater absurdity to human fears and hesitation.

His insignificance is the greatest comedy and this fuels his quest to do as he pleases and enjoy and experience everything this brief sojourn has to offer.

68-The Entrepreneur is no accident

The vast majority of Entrepreneurs are produced by their surroundings;, very few are born into this world, in the same way few are born with six fingers.

Entrepreneurs are made when they encounter privation in childhood – emotional and physical. They learn that love is not given freely, that they are at the whim of others possessed by madness and cruelty, that there is not enough material goods to provide for them, and so on.

As they mature and begin to distill the messages they receive about fairness and plenty, and compare this against the reality of their lives, this is when they start to change.

For those born into the minimum of safety and security the bumps along the road happen later, perhaps when they go away to college or enter the workforce.

All around them they see dissonant facts colliding with the messages they have absorbed. Most will try to make do, or alter their behavior to blend with the herd, but a select percentage will take a step back and consciously assess the situation.

They will conclude that in order to provide for themselves, in order to protect themselves from accomplished thieves and in order to achieve some degree of self-creation, that they have to discard the broad propaganda of a just and fair world and get down to the dirty business of taking what they want and need.

69-The Entrepreneur knows freedom isn't "free"

While this phrase is normally associated with the armed forces this saying has a deeper meaning for the Entrepreneur.

He knows that the era of easy freedom is over – business and government forces are too hungry for money and power to let people stroll through their lives without subtracting a heavy toll.

People are not free today because larger forces won't leave money on the table meaning they will mine every crevice of human behavior for profit.

The Entrepreneur knows he has to fight for positions and perks of power and enough money to be considered autonomous.

The poor are not free because they haven't figured out there is an intellectual, behavioral and financial component to obtaining and keeping freedom.

The Entrepreneur knows that he must fight to secure his freedom.

70-The Entrepreneur knows societal rage is born from envy

When the recriminations start bubbling about injustice in society – especially when it comes to outsized benefits accrued by a small number of players – the Entrepreneur understands the rage is not as much about the deed itself, but the awareness on the part of the angry that they did not have the courage to pull off the scam.

The indignant are propelled in part by self-loathing – they see they were not smart enough, or bold enough, to take the actions that led to the rewards.

So the anger is not so much about clawing back the spoils, or exacting punishment for the deed, so much as for showing the meek exactly what cowards they really are.

The Entrepreneur knows you can take their money, and you can take their freedom, even their lives – but it is dangerous to strip away their self-delusion.

71-The Entrepreneur remembers himself daily

Dreams die because they are slowly forgotten.

In the mix of the day, when answering challenges and small obstacles, the Entrepreneur sees the danger of his goal evaporating behind the noise.

That is why he takes a moment, or an hour, to remember himself.

To reassert his authority over his life.

To remember that he is the only judge over what he is to do.

To recall his power - and assert himself over the demands of the world.

To exercise his capacity for action and move toward his ultimate goal.

To see again his dream of freedom and autonomy from the ordinary.

To prove to himself that he is the only one who can make it real.

The Entrepreneur remembers himself exactly when it seems most difficult.

He keeps his dream alive simply by not allowing sleep to steal what he wants most.

72-The Entrepreneur assesses his progress

The Entrepreneur considers how much he has accomplished.

He remembers where he started, and what he thought of himself when he began.

He sees how much of his dream he has made real and how easy it was to make it happen.

The Entrepreneur takes into account the obstacles along the way and analyzes how to avoid or minimize them going forward.

He sees how he could have done more, and made bigger, faster strides.

He is satisfied with his victories and adjusts his aims to be larger than he could have imagined when he began.

The Entrepreneur looks at his habits and adjusts them for smoother productivity.

He is happy with what he has and is prepared to move again in the direction of bolder goals.

He has become himself and wants more of it.

73-The Entrepreneur mows his lawn and shovels the sidewalk

When the Entrepreneur finds himself in close proximity to others, he follows the rules of engagement.

He does what is expected of him to maintain relations and just a little bit more.

He is about his project and can't be bothered getting drawn into petty entanglements.

Feuds and spats are for the little people.

He will draw amusement when they try to drag him into arguments or talk about their small battles.

Rather than drain his energy, it gives him fuel - the field is wide open for him to work on his master plan.

He knows the long-term effect of his posture - he appears to be the steady rock of the neighborhood, someone that can be counted on. A voice of reason.

This estimation of him in the eyes of others gives him more power than the effort it took to smile and take the garbage cans out on time.

Therefore he views it as energy well spent, and a boon to his plan.

74-The Entrepreneur does not get thrown under the bus

The Entrepreneur knows people want to avoid

responsibility and blame others when things go wrong.

That is why he is always in front delivering his best.

He does this in a manner where everyone can see the effort, but without bragging.

The Entrepreneur documents his contribution and results.

When there are warning signs he raises them in a manner that is also documented.

Always, he is self-directed, creating results and monitoring the overall health of the situation.

Because he is aware of his situation, he knows when problems are coming.

He will attempt to head off failure by again, raising concerns and offering solutions.

When an inevitable failure occurs, he ensures he is part of the after action conversation.

Again, his goal is to deliver results above the baseline, and also to ensure the finger pointing doesn't waver in his direction.

Getting blamed for someone's failure is an easy way to lose progress through no fault of his own.

To the Entrepreneur this is unacceptable, so he is vigilant with not only his own work, but what is going on around him.

Again, the weakness of others can be parlayed into an advantage, which the Entrepreneur can accomplish simply by being competent and alert.

75-The Entrepreneur doesn't think he's greedy

The Entrepreneur's only goal is his own good.

He may have started with this proposition from a young age or come to realize it after years of untangling false morality.

Either way, he doesn't care what anyone else thinks.

Least of all whether or not someone considers him greedy.

The concept to a full-fledged Entrepreneur is odd.

Why would anyone be dedicated to anything but their own good?

He is aware, however, that most spend their lives being run by ideas placed in their head by others - that you should be compassionate and generous and so on.

So when these others come across him and his single-minded focus they can be taken aback.

The Entrepreneur knows they don't see his compassion or generosity - because he doesn't wave it like a banner.

He knows they see what they have been taught to see - something different than the norm - and something that should be judged and condemned (because that is also the norm).

So the Entrepreneur tends to his only business, which is himself.

76-The Entrepreneur breathes

The Entrepreneur's breath fuels his life.

He takes time daily to be aware of his breath - especially if he feels himself getting tense or even anxious.

He breathes deeply, through the nose, filling his body and emptying his mind.

He repeats this exercise ten times, every time he remembers.

He allows his mind to exist in the background as he pays attention to his body.

He continues breathing until he has felt the energy rush back into his system.

He continues until he is fully relaxed.

He allows the chatter in his mind to completely dissolve, until only his being remains.

He knows the breathing exercise has done its job when

his thoughts are content.

He may go back to what he is doing or simply let it rest for awhile.

He takes stock of where he is and where he is going.

The Entrepreneur learns how to use his breathe to remain aware, and productive.

He practices breathing several times a day, knowing that it is the one thing he has - and that his breathe alone will take him where he desires.

The Entrepreneur makes an ally of his breath and turns it into a formidable tool for living.

77-The Entrepreneur knows this contest is decided daily

People try to assert themselves over each other every day.

In this contest there is a winner and there is a loser.

If you are an employee earning a wage and the CEO makes 300 times your salary, you are losing.

If the city, landlord or bank decides to assess another fee or change the rules, you are losing.

The Entrepreneur knows this is often referred to as society or democracy but the scorecard remains.

The Entrepreneur takes offensive action. He wants to win.

He wants to win money, assets and transactions. He wants fine things and not replicas of what his parents had.

The Entrepreneur doesn't worry about battles where there's no margin in fighting - the cost of living will always go up by a thousand greedy hands, so he concentrates on money.

The Entrepreneur wants to assert himself over the marketplace. He wants to assert himself over the cost of living. The Entrepreneur asserts himself over programming and messaging that says he can't do something and that is perhaps the most important and yet invisible battle.

For the Entrepreneur understands that someone is always trying to assert themselves over somebody else. Because of this truth he dedicates himself to asserting his own desires over the world around him.

78-The Entrepreneur does not beg for what is his

The Entrepreneur assumes everything is his to possess experience or control.

All of it.

His view of himself is as absolute power over his life.

He sees the things outside of him as details.

The Entrepreneur moves to have what he wants. He studies the means and the effort and acquires it.

He will work and deal and maneuver.

But he will not beg.

The Entrepreneur picks it up by the handle and takes it.

79-The Entrepreneur contemplates his best interest

This sums up the Entrepreneur's philosophy and his daily mental practice.

"What is my best interest?"

Is it in my best interest to make a large sale today, to increase the reach of my business?

Is it in my best interest to concern myself with this issue (a neighbor, or colleague's problem)?

Etc.

When the Entrepreneur contemplates his best interest - daily, repeatedly, his life improves.

He is happier - even before he accomplished a thing.

He is calmer and has a smile on his face.

He moves through the world and realizes it is made for him.

When the Entrepreneur thinks of his best interest before making a move, or a decision, his mind is clear.

This is recipe for instant happiness, for the dissolution of worry, and makes doubt and indecisions disappear.

Contemplating his best interest is the core of the Entrepreneur's plan - it works the day he puts it into practice and gets stronger with time.

When the Entrepreneur finds himself tired or confused, he can reset himself by asking, what is in my best interest?

This method is the key to solving problems and getting better results.

It is simple, it is enjoyable and it works.

And you, who are an Entrepreneur and already living in a manner that suits your own desires, ask yourself, is this in my best interest? To follow my own interest?

At all times and above all else? You know it is so, and therefore you can renew your commitment to contemplating, and acting upon, your own best interest.

80-The Entrepreneur does not seek approval

When asked, most Entrepreneurs will respond they are working for their own goals, their own satisfaction.

In reality, this is very rare.

Entrepreneurs are human, and as such have many drivers, many unconscious that compel them toward their aims.

They may be looking to prove someone wrong, or be defiant, or win the love of someone, often a parent, who is no longer even on the scene.

Or they want to make a statement, or be famous or notorious, In the end, these are often futile and even self-destructive drivers.

Most often they result in the person not even achieving their aims.

The fact they are outward directed means they don't actually have the inner drive to accomplish the thing on their own.

What they did have was an emotional wound that was driving them, so all they are doing is acting out a perhaps childish response.

No, the mature Entrepreneur does it because it pleases him. Because it gives him what he wants. Because it makes him perform at a level that makes him feel powerful, or alive.

The real Entrepreneur does things because he wants to. Things he would do if no one was watching or if no one would ever know.

The real Entrepreneur pleases himself by serving himself.

81-The Entrepreneur forges this path to freedom

The Entrepreneur is not interested in a vague notion of freedom.

He is rational and therefore specific.

He wants freedom of his time, of movement and association.

To obtain this he knows there is only one path.

He resolves to draw freedom from his own talents, to apply his own effort to give himself the things he desires.

He surveys the landscape and devises a means to obtain it and them applies himself - without prayer to the gods or government or superstition.

He earns his freedom, first in his mind by deciding that he is free to exercise authority over his life, to recognize only himself and to serve his best interest.

And then he does the work with these tools of self-possession, to engineer the freedom he desires. This is his road. It is light and full of cheer because he has begun rightly.

He is free the moment he takes control of himself, and then further bolsters that state with his own gifts, his own action and his own fortitude. And thus, his freedom is sweet and elevates him to the status of a living god.

82-The Entrepreneur determines his value

For the Entrepreneur born in poverty, and who then awakens to the limitless value of his person, he faces this dilemma:

He has no money yet values himself as wealthy.

He then realizes his project – which is to accrue outward value to himself that is equivalent to his self-recognition.

The Entrepreneur understands that material poverty is the same thing as having no value as a person.

This is the formula the world uses. There is no use arguing with it.

Without wealth he is powerless and serves at the whim of others.

Worse yet, his life is in constant danger from the effects of poverty and slavery, either by disease, the behavior of those stuck in the same condition, or forces that do not value his right to existence.

The Entrepreneur is determined to extract value from the world that squares with his self-assessment.

There is no way around this dilemma. It is a problem the Entrepreneur is willing and eager to solve.

He knows his physical life depends on it, never mind his mental and emotional health.

And because he was born into poverty, yet gifted with the unlimited wealth of his person, he understands he was already granted enough power, to balance the scales.

83-The Entrepreneur eats what he kills

The Entrepreneur has decided that what he wants he must have – and he will take it.

This means acting, outside of his mind and his daydreams, and interacting with others who have what he wants.

It may simply be the money of others – and he will use the mechanisms available to transfer it to his account.

It may be power, and again this is the power to affect external affairs. If so, he seizes it.

The Entrepreneur may see an opportunity to leapfrog the competition, capturing their customers and destroying his rival's business in the process.

All this is nothing to him. For the Entrepreneur, he is not taking so much as giving what he wants to himself.

Because the Entrepreneur sees the world as inert, and without any masters but himself, he strides onto the field and gives himself what he desires.

The Entrepreneur's advantage is the way he views himself – as ruler of all he perceives – and his capacity to act as if everything exists for his pleasure.

He knows no one will give him what he wants, and that wishes and hopes are nothing but eulogies for the defeated.

The Entrepreneur, at one with himself, with his power and his desire, eats what he kills.

84-The Entrepreneur is the only god in town

The Entrepreneur comes into possession of himself when he accepts the enormity of his being - that he is a mind, an invisible force, and at the same time alive in a body.

He revels in contemplating the connection between his spirit and his flesh.

Yet the Entrepreneur is not a ghost - he does not think his mind came from, or is going somewhere else. It is embedded in a vehicle that is strictly single-use.

And he does not believe there are unembodied spirits floating around thanks to an undiscovered physics, ready to impart him wisdom, clues to wealth or revelations of the future.

The Entrepreneur considers the world has been made by a million minds that came before him, using their invisible spirit and their flesh, to shape the world into their image.

His mind rests easy in his body, knowing that he possesses the same power - to conceive something from the invisible and use his power to make it real. He has been granted dominion over the world.

The Entrepreneur has no need for any other god, for he is busy with the act of creating a new world, for his enjoyment and personal use.

85-To the Entrepreneur belongs the world

The Entrepreneur is his own power. All he recognizes is himself – he sees the laws and walls of the world and while he may go along with them, they do not own him.

He is the sole owner of himself – and all things outside of him are seen as things that he can own if he so desires.

The Entrepreneur does not belong to a foreign power, a company or a group.

Therefore the Entrepreneur, who is owner and not owned, can make anything he pleases.

He can take any action or conceive any thought.

Before he allows his mind to venture into fantasy, at all times he contemplates his power over himself, the ability to decide what to believe or with whom to associate.

He is fluid like a river that is always moving and yet always an identifiable thing. He lives in the world as all things do, but blesses himself with the exercise of his own power – over himself and his surroundings.

Because the Entrepreneur is the original and unique owner, he looks out at the world and decides that it is his to have, to possess and to use as he pleases.

86-The Entrepreneur knows fear is a construct

As a human animal the Entrepreneur experiences fear. But because so much of modern fears have little to do with real, physical threats, he knows it is manufactured in the mind.

The Entrepreneur uses fear to his advantage – he knows that by confronting, and examining its cause, he is at the doorway of understanding how his psychology works.

He will notice how certain people, or circumstances

trigger fear within him, and he can trace their root to a childhood or other formative event.

He confronts fears and recognizes how it is the primitive part of his mind giving up – based on an unconscious belief that he does not have the power to deal with the actual facts.

And once he has practiced this exercise a few times, he understands fear is a pattern that can be rewritten. The Entrepreneur has decided that he will recognize himself as the only power. That he will exercise his power and he will at all times enjoy his power.

So when the Entrepreneur is confronted with an experience of fear he will breathe and ask himself if there is an opportunity for him to exercise his power in a practical way – and each time he does so, he feels the fear recede, and dissolve, leaving only his power in its place.

For fun, the Entrepreneur will seek out experiences that would cause fear – to experience the thrill of applying his power of reason and self-determination over his primitive mind.

87-The Entrepreneur exercises his power in the marketplace

The Entrepreneur revels in the feeling of his power. He looks out at things that used to cause him worry, or even fear.

Very quickly the Entrepreneur's imagination turns to how to use his power for more than self-satisfied reflection.

He feels like a humming engine with the power of a thousand horses and wants to translate that into material results.

The Entrepreneur aims to use his power to remake the world around him – yes to earn and possess but mostly to build.

To take natural resources or human behavior, and shape them into something that never existed.

He wants to channel the inert and often invisible power outside of himself and create an edifice that takes on a life of its own.

The Entrepreneur turns his mind to business – ones that exist that he can remake or others that have never been attempted.

The Entrepreneur is pleased when he uses his own power, to create something that commands the attention and resources of others and consumes their attention as if he was present in front of each and every one of them.

The Entrepreneur enjoys the glory of business because it is an organic channel into which humans have exerted their own power since the beginning of civilization, each iteration building either on the achievement or the rubble of the last.

Commerce is where the Entrepreneur thrives because it is power in itself and in its operation – and he aims to apply his own power to this realm and make it known.

88-The Entrepreneur is a man of action

The Entrepreneur's desire to satisfy his own needs are all the training he requires.

He begins the day by celebrating his power over his own life.

His mind moves to consider the next action he will take to continue enjoying the life he has created.

His body is already in motion before the thought has been completed.

Action is his tonic and his reward for taking command of himself.

He relishes the feeling of moving through the tasks that make his vision complete.

He sees the results and enjoys what his actions have caused.

He sees the expression of his spirit at work in the world and is pleased.

By taking command of himself and executing vigorous action he remakes the world in his own image.

The Entrepreneur is sometimes amazed at how easy a life of constant action is – once he has fully accepted himself as the only power driving his unique existence.

89-The Entrepreneur closes the gap

When there is a difference between what he has and what he wants, the Entrepreneur closes the gap.

It is a simple matter. There is a distance between point A and point B and that is all he focuses on.

The Entrepreneur begins, as always, by meditating on his power. If it can be had, made or acquired, he affirms that he will use his power to make it so.

Then he analyzes the gap. If the difference is due to his own failure, he is honest with himself.

If the difference is due to a lack of effort, training or connections, he will be ruthless to ensure he obtain what he needs.

His focus is on closing the gap. It is only a minor difference and easily bridged.

The Entrepreneur knows many will live their entire lives in the gap, always wanting, complaining and despairing over their condition.

He is willing to make the extra effort, to improve his condition and prove to himself that he has the power to create the life he desires.

He knows that after he has built and crossed this bridge, that new adventures await that will be more thrilling, and easier to traverse. He will look back at these moments and understand that his effort and determination were the means by which he created a fulfilling life.

90-The Entrepreneur is outcome oriented

The Entrepreneur begins with the end in mind.

His vision is on completion – and the feeling of satisfaction that comes with achieving his aim.

The Entrepreneur acts as if he had already accomplished his task – because it is so in his mind. He moves as if he already possesses the reward that he has claimed and enjoys its fruits today, even if the journey in front of him is long.

The Entrepreneur knows that focusing on the outcome – and behaving as if the victory is won – is the means by which he learns the knowledge and skills necessary to make it so.

He is already bigger, and more powerful today by the use of this tactic.

He inspires belief around him – and gains assistance – by this method.

In this manner, the Entrepreneur begins each day by winning, and this gives him the energy and confidence necessary to make it to the end.

The Entrepreneur stays focused on the outcome, putting details such as challenges in their proper perspective.

He enjoys this approach as it makes all projects more fun and easier to complete.

The Entrepreneur's life is full of joyous outcomes, some that can already be seen, and others that exist in his mind, and which he is bringing to fruition today.

www.ingramcontent.com/pod-product-compliance
Lightning Source LLC
Chambersburg PA
CBHW071943210526
45479CB00002B/789